A PIECE *of* PARADISE

A STORY OF CUSTER STATE PARK

By Edward Raventon / Photography by Paul Horsted

FALCON™

HELENA, MONTANA

Library of Congress Cataloging-in-Publication Data

Raventon, Edward.
    A piece of paradise : a story of Custer State Park / by Edward
Raventon ; photography by Paul Horsted. — 1st ed.
        p.   cm.
    ISBN 1-56044-499-1
    1. Custer State Park (S.D.) — Description and travel.   2. Custer
State Park (S.D.) — Pictorial works.   3. Raventon, Edward — Journeys —
South Dakota — Custer State Park.   I. Horsted, Paul.   II. Title.
    F657.C92R38 1996
    978.3'95--dc20   96-7949
                                                                  CIP

Published by Falcon Press in cooperation with the Black Hills Parks and Forests Association.

First Edition

Manufactured in Korea.

$\mathcal{A}$CKNOWLEDGMENTS

Thanks to Karri Fischer and all the board members of the
Black Hills Parks and Forest Association. Their love for
Custer State Park and the Black Hills, more than any one
factor, made this book a reality. Thanks also to Ron Walker
and his staff of biologists at Custer State Park for taking the
time to answer all my questions and serve, when necessary,
as my guide. And finally a special thanks to Craig and Celine
Pugsley for the cold beer and the warm hospitality.

—Edward Raventon

$\mathcal{I}$*started* exploring Custer State Park nearly ten years ago. Working intensely on
this book for days and weeks at a time over the past eighteen months, I have continued my
exploration. I know it will go on well after the publication of this volume. There is always some-
thing new to discover here, as each hour, day, and season rolls by.

My goal has been to observe and capture some of the magical moments that occur each day:
the first light of dawn spilling across the prairie, a thunderhead boiling up over granite spires,

the look of curiosity on a bison calf's face, stars wheeling across the night sky. My hope is that the sum of these experiences and the resulting photographs, with Ed Raventon's text, will provide a glimpse at the variety of flora, fauna, and vistas found in this special place. From our introduction, the reader can start his or her own exploration of Custer State Park, or perhaps relive these and other discoveries.

Mountain-sized thanks are due to the many people who helped me with this project, offering guidance, support, and suggestions. In particular, I thank Craig Pugsley, visitor services coordinator for Custer State Park, and his family, who welcomed me into their home many times (enduring my five-in-the-morning departures for the wildlife loop). Thanks also to Kevin and Maggie Hachmeister, who shared their home and love of nature with me; to Karri Fischer and the board of the Black Hills Parks and Forests Association for their confidence to give me this project; to writer Ed Raventon for illuminating many aspects of Custer State Park (and for blazing such a path through the poison ivy in French Creek!); to Lori Iverson and Jim Borglum for their friendship and cool drinks on the porch of the State Game Lodge; and to Sally Svenson, park naturalist, for sharing her enthusiasm for nature and the park.

Special thanks are also due Al and Linda Riner, greatest in-laws in the world and residents of the Black Hills, for driving me to and from the airport, loaning me their car, and putting up with my erratic schedule; and finally to my wife, Camille Riner, for letting me leave for work a thousand miles away and always welcoming me home again with arms open. At this moment, we are transplanted in Michigan, but plan to return to South Dakota one day.

A closing note: I've noticed that sometimes people will see a picture in a book or magazine and believe they have to find that exact spot if their visit is to be complete, as if the book is an all-inclusive checklist. Let this book guide you, but realize that the story and photographs of every wondrous thing in Custer State Park could never be contained in a single volume—not even in a hundred volumes. The Giver of All Things continues to create many special places and moments that you may not find on these pages. Watch for these, all around you, as you wander through grass, glade, and granite.

—**Paul Horsted**

CONTENTS

INTRODUCTION

*N*ative peoples of many plains tribes regarded the Black Hills as a "Holy Wilderness," attributing mystical and regenerative powers to this range of dark mountains situated in the center of the Great Plains. Its interior parks and valleys were filled with lush grass and wildflowers. Pure, cold water gushed from countless springs to fill creeks and streams, while a host of wild creatures roamed through glades and vast pine and spruce forests that cloaked the high ridges and mountain peaks.

*T*hese earlier peoples were mostly nomads—hunters and gatherers who camped in the foothills of this great rock and forest enclave and who, on occasion, would venture to penetrate its mysterious core. With the coming of the trappers, miners, loggers, and agricultural settlers in the nineteenth century, a good deal of the Black Hills ecosystem was disrupted—so much so, and at such an alarming rate, that one man, Peter Norbeck, felt it imperative to restore one special part of the Paha Sapa wilderness to a natural state, and to conserve it for all generations.

*D*ue to Norbeck's foresight, Custer State Park was established in the early part of the twentieth century to preserve the intrinsic beauty of its landscape, along with all the natural relationships of plant and animal life that had once flourished here. In the end, Custer State Park resembles a piece of the old primal paradise regained, with the additional benefit of being open and accessible to all.

*T*his book, complemented by Paul Horsted's photography, is simply one person's record of a series of journeys into the heart of the "Holy Wilderness." Many others have gone before, looking for beauty, tranquility, inspiration, adventure, and renewal. It is all there and more. Use this book as a guide to the interior, and may your journey be filled with amazement, delight, and wonder.

—**Edward Raventon**
Spearfish, South Dakota

Remnants of a thunderstorm pass over the Black Hills.

I

S U M M E R   A N D   S M O K E

Lightning illuminates the night sky behind a pine-covered ridge in Custer State Park.

*I*t is early July, and the morning has been seasonably hot—90 degrees Fahrenheit at midday. By three o'clock in the afternoon, woolly white cumulus clouds have matured into massive, anvil-shaped thunderheads, while dark curtains of nimbus skirt the highest peaks of Custer State Park. Lightning flashes are followed by explosions of thunder that crack the dry air and resonate up distant canyons and gulches. The rumbling seems far off, but already the air tastes of rain sweetness.

Lulled by the promise of moisture, a hard crack of thunder splits the sky. The boom is so loud it shakes the State Game Lodge, where guests who have been casually visiting on the porch are stunned into silence. The hot, dry wind that was blowing from the south, feeding the convection of updraft currents, now shifts and blows from the northwest. The downdraft is brisk and refreshingly cool. Lightning flashes are accompanied by claps of thunder that roll and rumble through the wet, heavy air. Large drops of rain plop and splatter on the pavement in front of the lodge.

Near the Needles Highway, ten miles northwest of the Game Lodge, a bolt of lightning strikes an old ponderosa pine, blasting it into long, shivering splinters of raw wood. A small fire smolders, then flickers momentarily, in the surrounding duff. In minutes the wind stiffens, pushing an opaque veil of silver light that is in actuality a cold shower of rain. The downpour lasts for fifteen minutes before the rain veil passes eastward onto the parched plains, where it will stretch and fragment into purple virga that never touch the ground. It is a typical afternoon in early summer over the granite spires and

The intense heat of a direct lightning strike vaporized the moisture inside this ponderosa pine, blowing it apart; this time, the tree did not catch fire.

rolling pine and grass ridges of Custer State Park.

This time, the rain extinguishes the smoldering duff under the old pine. Nature took another course in Custer State Park on an early July day in 1988. The same stormy situation occurred without the blessed relief of water from the sky. The 1980s had been a decade of severe drought like few could remember in the Black Hills. Pine forests lay tinder dry for weeks. On the afternoon of July 4, 1988, a brewing storm spewed out a profusion of lightning strikes. On a remote granite ridge above Galena Creek, one bolt ignited a tree. Fire flashed, and no rain followed. By late afternoon the blaze had consumed fifty acres of timber. Within two hours, fanned by wild, hot winds, the raging conflagration had charred five hundred acres of timber.

By the next day, fire had roared into the high country at the head of Bear Gulch, in the northeast section of Custer State Park.

The State Game Lodge, Park Headquarters, and the Black Hills Playhouse were in imminent danger of destruction. Only a heroic effort by firefighters saved these historic structures. By evening, the lightning-started fire had burned six thousand acres.

On July 7, the afternoon wind shifted and pushed the still-hot fire up the east side of Mount Coolidge to within a few hundred yards of the mountain's historic fire tower. Again, destruction was narrowly averted. That evening, a rain shower, generated in part by the density of smoke and ash particles swirling in the air, cooled the conflagration enough to give firefighters an edge, and by the next day sixty percent of the blaze had been brought under control. By late Sunday,

A forest fire covering several hundred acres burns in the Black Hills.

Fire sweeps through a stand of ponderosa pine.

Photo courtesy of Custer State Park.

July 10, only hot spots remained. The fire, after six hellish days, had been contained.

This fire, known as the Galena Fire, burned nearly seventeen thousand acres inside Custer State Park, and another thousand outside the park boundaries. Inside the park, twelve thousand acres of pine were completely incinerated, while four thousand acres were heavily damaged. The hottest burn area occurred at the head of the middle and north forks of Bear Gulch, in the northeast section of the park, where temperatures during the fire hit a scorching 900 degrees Fahrenheit. No one could remember anything like it. A local newspaper clipping from 1889 noted that a great fire burned an estimated fifty thousand acres between Iron Creek and Squaw (Coolidge) Creek, covering much of the same area over which the Galena Fire raged.

Fire has always stalked the ponderosa pine of the arid West, making no exception for the Black Hills. It destroys and rejuvenates with abandon and nonchalance. In its wake, life sorts and sifts itself out again, reminding us that a much older order exists, one that even the wisest management can only partially control. Fire periodically clears the Black Hills of its burden of pine so that other wild plants and creatures may have their time, their place, and their season in the sun. ⚡

Because it was located in a low-lying moist area, a grove of aspen and pine survived a forest fire near Mount Coolidge, while the surrounding hillsides burned off completely.

Lush new growth in areas which have burned attract wildlife, such as bighorn sheep.

BEAR GULCH

On the ridges above Bear Gulch several years after the burn, the middle and north fork areas present a stark landscape of umber rock outcroppings that still host a bristle of black, burnt snags. Yet here a magnificent transformation is in process. The hillsides are verdant with stands of tall grass and thick patches of raspberry bushes, sunflowers, fireweed, goldenrod, and mint.

Once characterized by a dry streambed, Bear Gulch now hosts a continuous clear stream of pure water, due to the removal of trees that previously sapped its lifeblood. Elk, bison, and bighorn sheep have moved into the area to enjoy the water and the lush forbs and grasses; sparrows and larks native to prairies and open glades have come to make their homes here.

II

INYAN: THE FIRST MOVEMENT

The Cathedral Spires are part of the Inyan
granite core of the Black Hills.

Photo by Laurence Parent.

Two billion years ago, molten stone welled up from deep within the earth, eventually forming what geologists refer to as the crystalline core of the Black Hills. This great igneous core or batholith, estimated to be ten miles deep, makes up the center of the Black Hills. It is composed of ancient granites and schists. Traditional Lakota people sometimes refer to this hardened, igneous stone as Inyan—the Stone Nation. It is Inyan that figures prominently in the Lakota origin story, the first creation legend, whereby the Great Spirit gives movement to the Stone Nation People.

Over ensuing epochs, the rising and falling of shallow inland seas buried the Inyan core granite under huge deposits of sand mixed with iron. Later, warmer seas flooded the rock, hosting a vast array of evolving marine life, whose hardened shell bodies built up thick beds of buff-colored limestone. The great epochs of sand and iron deposition, followed by the later limestone-building eras, created the following rock strata, in order of oldest to youngest: Madison limestone, Minnelusa sandstone, Minnekahta limestone, and the red shale and gypsum of the Spearfish beds. All of these rock formations are, to varying degrees, exposed in Custer State Park.

Following this early period of sedimentary deposition, about sixty million years ago, a process known as the Laramide orogeny, or Rocky Mountain uplift, thrust the Black Hills ten to fourteen thousand feet upward, creating a dome 125 miles long (north and south) and 65 miles wide. Incessant forces eventually weathered and swept away the relatively soft sedimentary layers of rock covering the core at the center of the Black Hills, exposing the oldest, hardest granitic rocks. In slow degrees, the granite was sculpted by the wind, carved by water, and flaked by the sun to create the huge monoliths of today—Harney Peak and Little Devil's Tower—as well as the smooth, rounded spires and pipes known as the Needles and the Cathedral Spires.

Granite spires in the Black Elk Wilderness area near Custer State Park.

Photo by Laurence Parent.

Mystical encounters had special meaning for prehistoric peoples and, perhaps,
for people who recognize and appreciate them today as well.

———

III

THE PEOPLE

Among the traces left by prehistoric visitors to western South Dakota are pictures carved into cliff walls. Their original meaning can only be guessed at.

When, exactly, the first human beings entered the Black Hills is uncertain. Archaeological evidence suggests that aboriginal peoples hunted mammoths and prehistoric bison with deadly atlatls on the high plains west of the Black Hills as early as 11,500 years ago. At that time, the Black Hills was a cold, treeless environment covered with tough grasses and tundra.

During the Holocene period, beginning ten thousand years before the present, the North American climate warmed and moderated. With the warming, the Black Hills became more hospitable and attractive to a growing host of plants and animals, which in turn attracted nomadic peoples. These early tribal groups quarried stone for their dart points and wintered in the

Bison were one of the primary game animals sought by nomadic hunters.

relatively warm canyons of the southern Black Hills. On the smooth sandstone walls of the canyons, they left etched red paintings of elk and bison, along with more elusive pictographs that suggest their interest in mysticism and life regeneration.

Following the passing of the prehistoric big-game hunters and nomadic gatherers, succeeding waves of aboriginal tribes continued to use the Black Hills as a place of shelter and sustenance. Toward the end of the sixteenth century, groups of Apache, Kiowa, and Kiowa-Apache people used the Black Hills. Later, Pawnee and Ree peoples entered the Black Hills from the south and east. Shoshone bands ventured in from the great mountains and high, dry plains to the west, while Crows or Absarokas, along with Arapahos, came from the north to live and camp in these Hills. Eventually, the Cheyenne people arrived in the Hills from the northeast.

By the early part of the nineteenth century, a large, fierce, and well-armed warrior society from the east, the Lakota, drove all other tribes out of the area, establishing their dominance over the Black Hills and most of the surrounding plains country. Perceiving the Black Hills as a "holy wilderness" possessing mystical and powerful regenerative qualities, the Lakota even today hold them in sacred awe.

The Hills were soon entered by other peoples. Starting in the 1820s and continuing through the 1830s, French and American trappers made incursions into the Black Hills in search of beaver pelts. During the 1840s and 1850s, rumors of gold in the Black Hills became more frequent. None were conclusive, however, until the summer of 1874, when a military expedition led by then-Lieutenant Colonel George Armstrong Custer reached the heart of the Black Hills and camped in the vicinity of what would later become Custer State Park.

Custer reached French Creek, near the present western boundary of the park, on July 31, 1874. During his stay, his men explored the adjacent valleys and gulches. Shortly thereafter, his miners discovered placer gold in French Creek. The camp went wild. Charlie Reynolds, a Custer scout, was sent to Fort Laramie with dispatches concerning the findings of the reconnaissance. Reynolds was obliged to travel by night and lie in the grass by day for four days to escape detection by the Lakota, who were anxious and angry at the defilement and inroads white men were making into their *Paha Sapa.*

Not all the gold in the Black Hills is found underground.

Photo by John W. Herbst.

When news of gold in the Black Hills hit the national wires, it triggered a frenzy. People wanted to rush into the Black Hills, which at that time were designated by treaty as Indian lands. Up until that hour, time in the Black Hills had been measured by the cyclical turn of the seasons and the spiraling arc of stellar constellations. After the discovery of gold, time became linear. The year 1874 marked the beginning of changes that swept this island of granite and pine into the chronology of written history.

A waning moon precedes sunrise over a lone ponderosa pine.

IV

GOLD AND THE GORDON PARTY

*While much has changed in more than
100 years, many areas of the Black Hills
look much as they did when the Gordon Party
first entered the area in 1874.*

*O*n October 5, 1874, a small party of gold seekers, consisting of twenty-six men, one woman, and a boy, led by John Gordon headed west out of Sioux City, Iowa, for the Black Hills. They walked more than four hundred miles across the Nebraska prairie and the Dakota badlands. The trip was extremely hazardous and illegal since Indian treaty rights excluded whites from the region. Gordon successfully managed to elude both the U.S. Army and Indians.

On the morning of December 1, 1874, just east of the Cheyenne River, the small expedition caught their first sight of the Black Hills where they hoped to find their fortunes. A little over a week later, they made their first camp in the Black Hills near present-day Piedmont. From that point, they followed the well-defined wagon road made by the supply train of the Custer Expedition. For two torturous weeks they wound through dark canyons and snow-covered glades before reaching what had been Custer's camp near French Creek. When the party of prospectors finally arrived, on December 23, 1874, a mere five months after Custer's departure, they were exhausted and overjoyed.

Three days after their arrival, a snowstorm hit the camp, burying it under two feet of snow. The snow was followed by a week of high winds and frigid temperatures. In camp, huge bonfires were built to ward off the cold. In January 1875, the men constructed a stockade for protection against the Indians, setting sixteen-foot-long pine logs on end and burying their ends three feet into the ground. The stockade, made accessible by a huge double gate, also included four corner bastions and portholes placed every eight feet. Only one cabin was roofed with sod; all the others were roofed with logs split lengthwise, hollowed out concavely, then carefully fit together.

Gold panning commenced, and early in February 1875, Gordon departed on horseback for Sioux City "loaded with gold and mail." Twenty-three days later he reached the settlement, displaying a sack of gold dust that created a tremendous amount of excitement and igniting what would soon mushroom into a mad rush to the Black Hills.

Heavy snow was one of the hardships encountered by the Gordon Party in late 1874.

On April 4, 1875, two months after Gordon's triumphal return to Sioux City, the U.S. Cavalry evicted the Gordon Party from the Black Hills and escorted them to Fort Laramie, where they were subsequently released.

Although the army turned off the trickle, it was unable to stop the ensuing flood of gold prospectors which, during the fall of 1875 and the spring of 1876, inundated the Black Hills. Gold mining in what would later be Custer State Park proved more promising than profitable. Nearly every prospector deserted the region to head for the fabulously rich gold camps farther north in Deadwood Gulch. The gold prospectors paved the way for the second wave of immigrants, the farmers and ranchers who settled in to raise livestock in the rich valleys and meadows of this area.

Isaac Clark and his family were among the first settlers to arrive and make their home in the lush Squaw (Coolidge) Creek valley, near the present site of the State Game Lodge. In 1881, Isaac Clark and his son Bert reported killing four mountain lions in the area and selling the hides for ten dollars apiece.

More settlers continued to arrive, quickly hunting and trapping out many of the native animal species. By the early 1880s, little remained of the beaver, bison, elk, bear, mountain lion, and wolves that once flourished in the Black Hills.

Within a few years of the arrival of settlers and prospectors, herds of bison, elk, and other species were gone from the Black Hills.

The GORDON STOCKADE

In 1925, a group of Custer citizens rebuilt the old Gordon Stockade on its original site. In 1933, a dam was constructed by the Civilian Conservation Corps (CCC)

across French Creek, creating Stockade Lake. Additional work on the Gordon Stockade was done by the CCC in 1941.

Since 1985, Custer State Park staff members have offered a summer living history program. Park staff, in the dress of the 1870s, recreate the day-to-day lives of gold seekers. The living history program includes historic tours of the Gordon Stockade and demonstrations of gold panning, sluicing, and cooking over an open fire.

The sun sets beyond a glass-like Stockade Lake.

The Cathedral Spires tower above the surrounding forest.

V

PETER NORBECK'S DREAM

The Needle's Eye is one of the natural wonders of Custer State Park which Peter Norbeck made accessible to visitors by engineering a road through the area.

*T*he man who established Custer State Park — Peter Norbeck — was a visionary and a progressive, a man of the people who was well in advance of his own time. People who love the Black Hills today are fortunate that they had Norbeck working on their behalf.

Peter Norbeck was born on his family's homestead northeast of Vermillion, Dakota Territory, in 1870. The oldest of six children, he helped

run the family farm, attending grammar school sporadically for a total of about three months each year. He was well educated at home by both of his parents and managed to attend a few semesters at the University of South Dakota, where he studied language, composition, civics, and algebra. As a young man, Norbeck attained financial success through his well-drilling machinery. By 1905, Norbeck had twenty-five well-drilling rigs in operation across the state. Through his business dealings, he quickly became well known and respected by the pioneers of the region.

Norbeck naturally gravitated toward new ideas and innovative technology; he was also an adventurer. In the summer of 1905 he made the first trip by automobile from Fort Pierre, South Dakota, to the Black Hills in his new Cadillac. In that era there were no bridges or ferries across the Cheyenne River and other lesser tributaries. Norbeck at times resorted to driving over train trestles, hoping for the best. On other occasions, Norbeck's Cadillac had to be hauled out of mudholes by cowboys on horseback using lariats. All together it took Norbeck and his two traveling companions three days to reach the Black Hills; on their best day they covered 87 miles. By comparison, the same trip today takes a little over three hours.

Norbeck's trip west also marked the beginning of his long love affair with the Black Hills. By 1909, Norbeck, a man of integrity and substance, had become popular enough to be elected to the state senate. There, he skillfully began to apply his considerable mental abilities toward his dream of creating a wildlife preserve in the Black Hills. First he initiated a plan to consolidate into one large tract all the public school lands in the Black Hills. These lands had been given to the state by the federal government. President William Howard Taft approved the consolidation in February 1912. The following year, the South Dakota legislature passed a bill creating a state forest and game preserve in Custer County and appropriated $15,000 to begin fencing an initial area of 48,000 acres.

Norbeck's dream was becoming reality. Elk from Idaho and Wyoming were the first animals to arrive at the Custer preserve. Twenty-five elk were placed in a new seven-hundred-acre enclosure in the spring of 1914. In December of the same year, thirty-six bison arrived from "Scotty" Philip's ranch outside Fort Pierre. It took twelve days to haul the bison in specially built trucks from the Hermosa stockyards nine miles away.

It is hard to imagine the amount of time

Some of Custer State Park's 1,400 bison rumble across the prairie. Bison were reintroduced to the park in 1914.

A mule deer animates a meadow along the Needles Highway.

and effort involved in these tasks, regarded as relatively simple today. Eighty years ago, creating and maintaining large herds of native Great Plains ungulates in a wild, natural setting was largely experimental and had few precedents. National parks existed and included wildlife, but the creation of a state game park from scratch, especially one of the dimensions Norbeck envisioned, had never been done. As South Dakota governor in 1916, Norbeck worked continuously to develop the wildlife park. That same year he saw the first pronghorn added to the game preserve, and worked—when his schedule permitted—to help fence the preserve, all the while negotiating with landowners whose adjacent property he felt was necessary to enlarge the park.

Along with pronghorn, beavers were reintroduced during this early period.

The winding Needles Highway is a delight to the eye in any season.

All of the wildlife species slowly began to increase their numbers, so that by 1919 there were 70 bison, 400 elk, and 10 pronghorn. Beginning in the 1920s, a small zoo was constructed, housing black bears, coyotes, badgers, marmots, a red wolf, a gray wolf, foxes, bobcats, raccoons, squirrels, and porcupines, along with various fowl, water birds, and birds of prey. The zoo would not fit long-range plans for the park as a natural setting for native wildlife and would be discontinued in 1970.

Norbeck firmly believed that the Cathedral Spires, the Needles, and Harney Peak should be made more accessible to the

The road couldn't go over this rock outcropping near the Needle's Eye, so Norbeck's engineers blasted a passage through the rock.

visiting public. To that end he enlisted the help of Park Superintendent C. C. Gideon and a bright, innovative civil highway engineer named Scovel Johnson, asking them to determine if it was possible to construct roads in this steep, mountainous terrain. In the early 1920s the three of them spent days riding horseback and walking over the rugged area in the vicinity of the Needles and Harney Peak. Norbeck wanted a road into the area that would reveal the tranquil and beautiful scenery without becoming a speedway or an imposition on nature.

Eventually a fourteen-mile route penetrating the very heart of the granite uplifts was mapped out. Johnson designed a road that would begin at 4,250 feet elevation, near the State Game Lodge, and slowly wind its way up to 6,250 feet, skirting the foot of the Needles and the shore of Sylvan Lake. Using 150,000 pounds of dynamite, he also blasted two tunnels along the way, creating one of the most scenic drives in the Black Hills: the Needles Highway. Johnson's work on the Needles Highway was a triumph of artistic development that made, as he put it, "the miniature kingdom of perpendicular cliffs and canyoned waterfalls" accessible.

After the Needles Highway was completed, Norbeck and Johnson tackled the Sheep Mountain Road. Known today as South Dakota Highway 87, the Sheep Mountain Road runs parallel to the western edge of Custer State Park. It coursed along the upper edges of high ridges before winding down through prime bison grazing areas and ultimately linking Custer State Park with Wind Cave National Park. A branch of the road spiraled around the steep west side, leading to the fire tower on Sheep Mountain, which was later renamed Mount Coolidge.

The third major highway in the park is the Iron Mountain Road, connecting the park with Mount Rushmore. It too was built with regard to preserving the pristine quality of the park. A lover of wilderness, Peter Norbeck believed that park visitors should actually get out of their cars and walk the roads, or at the very least drive them no faster than twenty miles per hour. Building the Iron Mountain Road was every bit as challenging as constructing the Needles Highway. There were to be three tunnels blasted through granite, with an additional complication: Norbeck wanted the tunnels to frame the four faces on Mount Rushmore. In order to accomplish this feat, superintendent C. C. Gideon was forced to figure out a way to loop and incline the road in order to traverse the great shifts in elevation. He devised a bridge that was, as he put it, "neither straight, level, nor flat, but a triple, corkscrew spiral." Three of these bridges had to be custom-designed for the road. They incorporated nine thousand pounds of steel beams plus long, specially cut logs for supports. The Iron Mountain Road, with its three pigtail bridges and three framing tunnels, was completed in 1933.

With his enormous influence, first as South Dakota governor and later as a U.S. senator, Norbeck guided almost every major aspect of Custer State Park's development. The completion of the Iron Mountain Road was the last park development project he would live to see. He died quietly three years later at his home in Redfield, South Dakota, having lived to see his dream become a magnificent reality.

A single ponderosa pine decorates a prairie ridge.

A Tribute *to* Two Statesmen

In 1919, Governor Peter Norbeck, known as the father of Custer State Park, signed legislation that created an area in the southern Black Hills where tranquility and wilderness could flourish. Later, as U.S. senator, he was instrumental in the creation of Mount Rushmore National Memorial and Badlands National Park. His commitment to park development, both on a state and national level, and his love of the Black Hills continued throughout his public and private life.

Governor George S. Mickelson, regarded by many as a modern-day Peter Norbeck, shared many of the same convictions as his visionary predecessor. From the early days of his administration in 1988, when he initiated a multi-million dollar park restoration and improvement plan, until his tragic death in 1993, he never wavered in his steadfast support of Custer State Park. Like Norbeck, he imposed only one uncompromising requirement: all planned development of improvements had to be compatible with the natural resources the park was initially established to protect. Mickelson's love for the park was evident in his thoughts, in his actions, and in his smile whenever he spoke of the park.

It is with deep gratitude and appreciation that we pay tribute to their vision, their belief, their sensitivity, and their commitment to protecting and maintaining a small piece of paradise called Custer State Park.

Rollie Noem, Director
Custer State Park
March 1995

In a time exposure of several hours, the earth's rotation creates star trails that circle the North Star over the Needles area of Custer State Park.

VI

Sunday Gulch on the Solstice

Ferns frame a waterfall along the
Sunday Gulch Trail.

*S*erenely cloaked in a deep green forest of pine and spruce, it is easy to be lulled into believing that this is always how the Black Hills have appeared. In fact, the Black Hills have progressed through many transformations over eons of time. Several waves of plant immigrants have passed over it. Some plants, such as the ferns and horsetails, are left from ancient times, while others, such as spruces, appeared at the end of the Ice Age, and remain in a niche in the great ponderosa pine forest that followed the warm weather north from the mountains of Mexico a short five thousand years ago.

The mix of vegetation tells a fascinating story in the Black Hills. The region is considered a crossroads for four major biological communities: eastern deciduous forest, Great Plains grassland, Rocky Mountain forest, and boreal forest. A spectacular place to view some of this diversity is along Sunday Gulch Trail, which begins near the former site of the old Sylvan Lake Lodge on the southwest side of the

The Sunday Gulch Trail beckons the hiker into its steeply descending path beneath tall granite cliffs.

———

Sylvan Lake dam.

At summer solstice, the longest day of the year, I walk Sunday Gulch, treated to one of those delightfully cool June days for which the park is justifiably famous. Mild temperatures in the mid-sixties combine with cumulus clouds, and a gentle breeze lightly ripples the water. On the trail, I pass through a three-foot-wide, fifty-foot-long fracture in a massive, pink granite wall. Large boulders wedged into the top of the fracture create an interesting tunnel effect. Below the dam grow handsome stands of some of the most common native Black Hills trees, including stately, old Black Hills spruces, ponderosa pines, and paper birches, along with a luxuriously thick stand of willows just below the spillway.

From that point, I drop with the creek, descending into a deep, narrow gorge where it winds through a jumble of huge boulders and tall trees. The beauty and serenity of this part of Sunday Gulch is without parallel—reminiscent of the fanciful Tibetan valley of Shangri-la, where the concept of linear time only rarely intrudes. High, rounded walls of stucco-textured granite, shaded in mosaics from a soft, pink blush to the dun gray of elephant hide, rise up beside me on both sides of the gulch. The variance in color is the result of ages of weathering; the pink spots, which appear as wounds in the elephant hide, are relatively recently exposed areas where the granite has shed its outer layers.

The creek gurgles pleasantly around all this magnificent geology, watering a host of lush, native trees and blooming shrubs, including serviceberries, choke-cherries, gooseberries, wild roses, red-osier dogwoods, and elder-berries. In this early flowering time of the year, each shrub adds its own fragrance to the cool, moist air, creating a delicate perfume.

I watch the play of sunshine streaming through tall, elegant trees. They are of varied species, both deciduous and coniferous, and occupy various levels of the gulch, creating unusual visual perspectives and moods. One side of the gulch might feature a mesmerizing sway of dappled light dancing through birch trees, while just below it, deep shadows cast by great boulders and high canyon walls hold cool and shady repose. The light-dark chiaroscuro contrast works to vividly highlight natural forms in shadow against the dazzle of verdant colors.

At streamside, among the shrubs,

Chokecherries are among the many native shrubs found along Sunday Gulch Trail.

massive shaded boulders with their backs facing north are covered with thick, green velvet pads of moss and crusty mats of lichen. Other boulders and large sections of canyon wall that spend most of the day in direct sunlight display neon orange and lime green lichen patches, giving the entire gulch eye-dazzling accents.

The final sense is aural. I listen to gentle rivulets of pure, fresh water burble over miniature waterfalls, finding their way into little swirling pools and smooth boulder grottos. Walking this part of the trail with its ingeniously placed handrails allows me to navigate right down the backs of the boulders and enjoy every nuance this tranquil and Edenic hideaway offers.

About a mile below the trail's entrance, Sunday Gulch Creek exits its granite enclave and makes a steep descent down through an old-growth stand of spruces hung with old man's beard. This stringy, bluish green plant

A wood lily accents the forest floor.

is an arboreal lichen that hangs most commonly from spruce trees, giving them a tinsel-draped appearance. The lichen-draped spruces, with low, thickly whorled branches and dense needle arrangements, tend to grow tall and close together, creating a dense canopy that shades and discourages other plant competitors. The deep shade cast by the dark spruces over exposed, gnarled roots and furry, moss-covered boulders creates that rich half-light of the forest primeval. It is a dim, shadowy world where my imagination leads me to expect delicate fairies, wood dryads, rock trolls, and water sprites.

Continuing down the gulch, I cut through drier surrounding terrain, more typical of the greater Black Hills ecosystem, which is often described as mesic, or dry. The lush plant life that is nurtured by the stream and protected by walls of granite begins to give way to plants that can tolerate a harsher, desiccating environment. About an eighth of a mile after emerging from the granite gulch, the valley opens up. Spruces and birches remain close to the stream and dominate the cooler north-facing slopes, while ponderosa pines cover the south-facing, high, dry inclines.

Farther down the trail, a couple of pitch stumps and logs, including a huge, old,

Black Hills spruce trees tower over a hiking trail.

fire-scarred ponderosa pine, bear witness to a fierce fire that roared through here perhaps a century ago. Beyond this old tree and around the next bend, a stand of ponderosa on a granite outcrop, protected from hot ground fires, has managed to attain old age.

From this high, rocky ridge, the trail again drops to streamside. The banks here are alluvial and thickly covered with lush stands of ferns and equisetum. Both of these plants are ancient and primitive. Ferns and their allies developed and proliferated during the Carboniferous era, 350 million years ago. For 70 million years they lived and died in tremendous abundance. True to their ancient origins, they live close to the water.

The stream again enters a small granite gorge. As the trail parallels the stream course, it meanders through a mixed forest of spruces, pines, and broad-leafed trees. From this point on, the trail winds its way back up to the top of the gulch, through a dry, scrubby forest comprised mostly of stunted spruce and pine. There are good views of granite ridges, but they pale in comparison to the upper part of Sunday Gulch, with its vibrant mosaic of shifting forms, textures, lights, and colors.

SYLVAN LAKE *and* LODGE

In 1890, Theodore Reder visited a lovely little valley hemmed in by smooth granite walls. He noticed that a creek drained the west side of the valley via a crevice in a huge, solid outcropping of granite. Believing a lake could be created behind the wall of granite, Reder filed ten mineral claims on the property in 1891. The following year, he began filling the crevice with concrete, creating a dam thirty-three feet high.

In 1893, Reder and his family built a handsome Victorian hotel near the south end of the dam. The hotel proved an ideal place for relaxation and quickly grew in popularity. Many visitors came to fish, swim, and enjoy leisurely strolls around the lake, while more adventurous visitors took longer hikes down Sunday Gulch and up to Harney Peak. Notable visitors in those early days included William "Buffalo Bill" Cody and Presidents Theodore Roosevelt and Calvin Coolidge.

In June 1935, Reder's grand old wooden structure burned to the ground. The new Sylvan Lake Lodge was built in 1938, higher up the mountain, overlooking the lake.

The Victorian-style Sylvan Lake Hotel and dance pavilion, built in 1893, accented the shores of Sylvan Lake until they burned to the ground in 1935.

Photos courtesy of Custer State Park.

Distant ridges of the Black Hills are bathed in the golden light of evening in this view from atop Little Devil's Tower.

PERCHED *on* LITTLE DEVIL'S TOWER

A tranquil moment at Sylvan Lake.

I had hoped to be on the trail to Little Devil's Tower by sun-up, but by the time I had breakfast, lingered over a second cup of coffee on the verandah of the State Game Lodge, and drove up to the trailhead near Sylvan Lake, it was already midmorning. The sky was overcast and quiet; the morning seemed late in starting also. Only the plaintive whicher-whicher-wee of a ruby-crowned kinglet punctuated the silence. His sweet, modulated song reminded me I had no need to rush.

The trail to Little Devil's Tower begins along an ephemeral stream that feeds Sylvan Lake. In summer, it trickles between banks thickly spread with tall stands of cow parsnip and sweet cicely. Large clones of dogbane appear in the small meadows and clearings,

White aspen trunks contrast with the forest greens along the Little Devil's Tower Trail.

accented by patches of wild white geraniums. At 6,200 feet, the forest comprises a typical mix of white spruce, ponderosa pine, paper birch, and aspen.

Aspen—all of my senses find aspen groves enormously attractive. My hands like the feel of their smooth white bark with its powdery, talcum texture. The symmetry of their soft, green, heart-shaped leaves appeals to my eye and turns out to be the perfect design for providing a soothing, rustling whisper when stroked by a gentle breeze. In late September, it is their leaves turning to brilliant yellow-gold and burnished reds that conclusively announces the arrival of autumn

in the Black Hills.

Along the trail is a small, old grove of aspen whose bark is unusually mottled with dark, rough, scabby patches and knobs. The bark of older aspen is often fissured and split. It is a good indication of age, regardless of girth and height. This grove appears to be an old one.

Aspen are short-lived and need fire or an active colony of beavers to periodically harvest the big stems. This natural thinning stimulates them to sucker. While the leaf-bearing stems have a life span that rarely exceeds seventy years, the rootstocks may remain vital for centuries. At any rate, this elderly grove has no smooth, pretty faces of youth.

Across the trail from the aspen, the stream winds through a thicket of choke-cherries and willow. A thin ribbon of meadow separates the aspen on the drier, rockier slope to the north from this riparian thicket. The

Black-eyed Susans accent the lower stretch of the trail to Little Devil's Tower.

meadow, still wet from last night's dew, sends forth a horde of hungry mosquitoes to meet me as I squat to take pictures of insects and flowers.

Farther up the trail, a century-old spruce lies, partially uprooted, twisted, and shattered, a victim of a particularly ferocious wind storm. Beyond the splayed spruce, low ridges of granite rise to the north with outcroppings shaped like huge billowy bread loaves.

As the slope and trail steepen, the ground turns dry and rocky. Spruce trees drop out of the forest, leaving only ponderosa pine and a handful of aspen to colonize the mineral soil. At the ridge summit, the trail drops through a wide fracture in a block of granite. The rock is shot through with tiny sheaves of glistening mica. Over thousands of years, the weathering process has peeled mica shavings off the rock face; they now litter the trail, creating a glittery path that sparkles in the sunlight.

On the shaded north-facing side of the ridge, the granite face is covered with patches of green, crustose lichens, appearing like large liver spots on the rock. Growing in the narrow crevices are small rock ferns, tiny sprigs of fringed sage, and delicate purple shooting stars. The foot of this lovely rock

A panoramic view near the summit of Little Devil's Tower.

garden is anchored by carpets of green moss.

After threading my way along a steep slope through stands of stunted, twisted pines and an understory of ground juniper, I catch my first glimpse of the monolith that is Little Devil's Tower. In less than a quarter of a mile, I arrive at the foot of the Tower and access it through another wide crevice in the granite. At the head of the passage, a small ladder allows me to climb up another side fracture that leads to the summit.

Growing in the talus along this fracture are limber pines, rare to the Black Hills. Limber pines prefer dramatic, windswept ridges and are the last gnarled trees you can expect to find growing at timberline. Uniquely adapted to endure deep, heavy, wet snows that might ordinarily break a spruce or ponderosa, limber pines, as their name suggests, bend and flex. They endure in this beautifully remote and austere corner of the Black Hills, raising their voices to a high-pitched keening when the wind blows through them.

Beyond the limber pines is the bald granite summit of Little Devil's Tower. The ancient bedrock is veined with thick sills of rose quartz and peppered with pegmatite. It

48

is the very heart of what was once the molten core of the earth. The view from the Tower's summit is spectacular. To the north, a deep gorge is filled with a vast unbroken forest of verdant spruce and pine, beyond which looms the great granitic body of Harney Peak. The old fire lookout tower on Harney Peak stands on a pediment of rock like a small medieval castle. Using binoculars, I can pick out mountain goats standing just below it.

Below me, and to the southeast, the Cathedral Spires stretch out like a row of pipes attached to a great organ, the massive keys and pedals obscured by the forest. I imagine the music that booms from these pipes as celestial, with long, deep, resounding tones. As I turn and face north, I discover a small grassy area just below me. Enclosed by rock outcrops, it offers shelter from the wind. A few plants have also found this shelter, including a stunted ponderosa pine, currant bushes, cinquefoil, raspberries, and shooting stars. Swifts dive overhead while chipmunks dart about the cracks and crevices in the rock.

A journal stuck in a crevice records the thoughts and feelings of sojourners who have tarried here before me.

The summit of Little Devil's Tower offers a breathtaking view as the moon rises over the Cathedral Spires.

Saturday, April 16

Truly a sacred spot;
Bless Mother Earth
for such beauty —
Listen to the wind
and hear what she speaks.

— Shelly M.

Sunday, April 17

Scattered clouds
and warm sunshine —
Breathtaking view;
sky forever;
trees, rock and patches of snow —
Praise God for His Creation.

— Scott and Jayneann

Little Devil's Tower is indeed an awesome perch to alight upon.

Sunset shadows a hiker against the granite formations near the top of Little Devil's Tower.

The Cathedral Spires and Limber Pine Natural Area

The summit of Little Devil's Tower and the immediate area around the Cathedral Spires are the only places in the Black Hills that limber pines grow. In 1966, the USDA Forest Service counted 167 limber pines in this area; a more recent count has added another 100 trees to their population. Prompted by the trees' rarity in the Black Hills, the Forest Service, in conjunction with Custer State Park, set aside 640 acres in 1979 as the Cathedral Spires and Limber Pine Natural Area.

Most of the limber pines, however, grow only on a small ten-acre site at an elevation of 6,600 feet. They are scattered over the summit and steep west-facing slopes of Little Devil's Tower. The mean age of limber pines in this area is 123 years, with the oldest tree aged at 192 years.

At the end of the Ice Age, ten thousand years ago, limber pines were numerous and grew in large forests at the edge of the glaciers that covered the Big Horn and Laramie Mountains down to 6,500 feet. They probably stretched in broken groves 150 miles east across the Wyoming plains to the Black Hills. As the climate warmed and the glaciers receded, the pines disappeared from the plains and retreated high up into the Laramie and Big Horn Ranges. While they are still abundant in these two Wyoming mountain ranges, they have all but died out in the Black Hills—all except for this particular stand, which managed to persist and survive.

MOUNTAIN GOATS

A unique animal with no near relatives on this continent, the mountain goat is not really a goat. Instead, it is a distant relative to the Old World antelope. It is believed that the animal we call a mountain goat originated in Asia and crossed the Bering land bridge 600,000 years ago.

Mountain goats are not native to the Black Hills, but were transplanted here from Alberta, Canada, in 1924. The hooves of these handsome, snowy white creatures are split into two toes and have spongy traction pads that help them grab hold of even the most slippery surfaces. Preferring the highest, most inaccessible peaks and terrain where they like to ruminate and search out natural salt licks,

mountain goats are most often sighted in the vicinity of Harney Peak, the Cathedral Spires, and Mount Rushmore.

VIII

Up on Harney Peak

Harney Peak looms out of the mist of early morning.

During summer, when afternoons are hot and dry, cumulous clouds often form over Harney Peak. They build and glide effortlessly through the sky. By late afternoon, as I begin my ascent of the legendary mountain, low thunder rumbles in the distance. The errant, dark clouds occasionally sprinkle a cool rain across the forest.

A short rest beneath a grove of pines allows me to relax and inhale

deeply the pungent aroma of hard, sun-baked rosin. It is the signature fragrance of the high, dry West, a pure, sweet incense.

In the highest reaches of the Black Hills, ponderosas dominate the area at elevations of 3,500 to more than 7,000 feet, while Black Hills spruce prefer the shaded canyons and north-facing slopes above 5,000 feet. Ultimately, it is the ponderosa pine that defines the term *forest* in the Black Hills.

Watching sunlight stream through the pine canopy while a wind rustles boughs and

A least chipmunk is one of the creatures that makes its home in the forests of the Harney Range.

needles reminds me of the naturalist John Muir's thoughts on ponderosa pine. "Of all the pines," he wrote, "this one gives forth the finest music." Wind more than any other element spreads ponderosa seeds and helps propagate new generations, but caches of buried seeds inadvertently overlooked by nutcrackers and chipmunks give life to some of the best seedling stands.

After running along a dry, pine-covered ridge for about a mile, the Harney Peak trail drops down a north-facing slope through dark groves of spruce and paper birch. The change is dramatic. In the course of a few steps, the forest world changes from one of dry rock and desiccation to lush greenery, moisture, and cool, deep shade. The forest is now dominated by boreal elements—spruce, aspen, and birch—while boulders and rocky slopes are enveloped in thick carpets of mosses and liverworts. Interspersed amidst a thick tangle of downed timber, the under-story supports mats of tiny, ground-hugging bunchberries, kinnikinnick, and slender wild sarsaparilla.

At the bottom of the ridge, the trail crosses a small creek, forks, and gradually ascends in a northerly direction. Granite pinnacles, peaks, and spires rise up through the forest. Like long, sleek spear points, tall,

*A nanny mountain goat and her kid find
safety and a resting spot high atop
a granite formation.*

magnificent specimens of spruce stand out in dark, dignified contrast against a softening, sunlit forest and a deepening blue evening sky.

Ascending switchbacks lead from moist shaded areas to dry, rocky slopes. As quickly as they appeared, all the northern elements give way to pines again. I am in the heart of the forest. Serenely quiet, untrammeled, and uncut, it feels enormously pure and reassuring.

Slowly, the trail switches up through doghair stands of ponderosa and thickets of stunted spruce, growing progressively steeper until it finally reaches the east-west summit ridge of Harney Peak. It is now evening. Most of the clouds created during the heat of the afternoon have dissipated. Long, orange rays of sunlight stream through the pines, creating deep shadows and a rich melancholy mood. The rhythm of life slows for a moment to reflect upon itself, before evening spreads its cloak.

Up on Harney Peak, views sweep in all directions. Close by loom the elegant Cathedral Spires and Little Devil's Tower, along with a host of unnamed smaller granite monoliths and spires that rise as round pediments from an unbroken sea of evergreens. Far to the west stretch the long, straight ridges of the limestone plateau. Terry Peak, Custer Peak, and Bear Butte stand out on the horizon. Closer in, the flat white back of Mount Rushmore shines in the evening sunlight. Beyond the Red Valley at the edge of the Black Hills, the white badlands

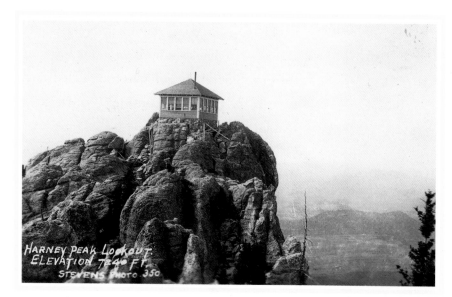

The original wooden lookout high atop Harney Peak.

Photo courtesy of Custer State Park.

shimmer in the haze.

The top of the mountain, at 7,242 feet above sea level, is the highest point in the Black Hills. Harney Peak is one huge monolith of granite, with patches of orange and lime green lichens decorating its knobby surface. In many places fractures have split the granite apart, creating deep vertical crevices. It is a powerful place. The famous Oglala medicine man Black Elk called it "the center of the world." He venerated this mountain. Many times during his long lifetime he came up here to pray to his Six Spirit Grandfathers.

It's about eight o'clock in the evening when the sun slides behind a long bank of clouds on the southwestern horizon, forcing

an early twilight that lights up high sweeps of cirrus to the north. A strong wind howls through the gaping window casements of the fire tower. There is just enough time to get back before total darkness makes traveling this rough trail hazardous.

Hiking briskly down the mountain through the growing shadows of evening, I remember the account of George Custer and his visit to Harney Peak. On July 31, 1874, Custer and a group of his men climbed the summit. They arrived in the evening and were reported to have "enjoyed the panorama of the Black Hills and surrounding plains." Their descent was made in the ensuing darkness; they stumbled over fallen logs and crashed through dense, tangled brush down

the steep hillsides. In one place, men reported having to hold their horses' tails for footing as they plunged through murky sloughs. All arrived back at camp, near the vicinity of the present-day town of Custer, after one in the morning, "enthusiastic about the journey in spite of the difficulties."

Since it is late, there are no other hikers on the trail. The plaintive calls of ruby-crowned kinglets emanate from deep forested shadows to keep me company, along with an occasional deer coming out to feed. With a fast yet unhurried pace, I reach Sylvan Lake just as the soft, warm glow of summer twilight completely gives way to the coolness of starry darkness.

The Harney Peak ranger tower with its sweeping views of the Black Hills and eastern plains.

Two hikers pause to enjoy the view of the Cathedral Spires.

VALENTINE T. McGILLICUDDY, INDIAN AGENT

In 1940, the Civilian Conservation Corps (CCC) built a handsome stone fire lookout tower atop Harney Peak. A bronze plaque set in stone here commemorates Valentine T. McGillicuddy with the words, "Wasicu Wakan, 1849-1939." The term *Wasicu Wakan* roughly translates from Lakota as "great" or "revered white man."

McGillicuddy was a doctor who accompanied the Newton-Jenney Geological Expedition to the Black Hills in 1875. Sympathetic to the Indian plight, McGillicuddy assumed the position of Indian agent at the Pine Ridge Reservation. His honesty and integrity won him the respect of the majority of Sioux Indian people.

Following government service, McGillicuddy went into private business in Rapid City for a few years. He eventually moved to California and died there in 1939. Although he never returned to the Black Hills, his cremated ashes did. Following his wishes, his remains were placed on Harney Peak. 🦬

*High summer in
the French Creek
Natural Area.*

IX

SOJOURN *down* FRENCH CREEK

In a remote stretch of French Creek, the stream
flows gracefully over granite boulders.

It is windy and warm the summer morning Paul Horsted and I start out to explore the French Creek Natural Area from the west end. This designated natural area comprises a twelve-mile corridor encompassing French Creek. There is no marked trail through it, and very few hikers attempt to walk the whole distance, perhaps, with good reason, as I was about to discover.

French Creek cuts a meandering, easterly course through the heart of Custer State Park. Gently flowing through granite canyon walls covered with bright patches of lichens, the upper stream nourishes a lush riparian plant community of sedges, bulrushes and ferns. Luxuriant, green, waving mats of flowering crowfoot grow in murky water, sheltering minnows and aquatic insects. In deeper pools, trout dart above the heads of slow-moving crawdads. Along the trail, huge bumblebees gather nectar from large thistle blossoms while butterflies skip and dip over meadow rue and dogbane.

During the first mile, signs of bison appear in the form of scarred, "horned-up" trees. Platoons of stately, old yellow-barks guard the stream at various bends. The forest floor is decorated with large clusters of wild white geraniums—and pernicious stands of poison ivy.

The first few miles of the trail have an abundance of logs and stones that facilitate a dry creek crossing. These amenities

A yellow swallowtail butterfly drinks nectar from a shell-leaf penstemon.

A bumblebee stops for food from a thistle.

disappear the deeper we penetrate into the natural area. At creek crossing number twenty-three, we are forced to remove our boots to keep them dry, and wade across. The cold water and soft chara refresh our hot feet. For the next few crossings, we dutifully remove our boots, but soon boot removal has become a chore and we plunge in, boots and all.

At a point west of midway, a spur from Fisherman's Flat marks the end of the well-defined horse trail we have been following. From here, we pick our own way downstream, often climbing over and around huge boulders and through dense thickets of poison ivy. Each new bend provides a different navigational challenge. Occasionally flats of tall pines and oaks appear, but more often we must pass over and through boulder fields choked with knee-high poison ivy. Never have I encountered such a rank and prolific growth of this noxious plant.

As the creek makes a more precipitous descent, small waterfalls appear. At one of the falls, hopelessly clogged with a knot of small boulders and thick tangles of driftwood, a sleek, wet mink darts about with an astounding agility. He appears twice for a second or so only five feet in front of us.

From these small waterfalls it is a scramble over boulders to the Narrows. Aptly named, the Narrows is the point where French Creek bends and cuts through a high, steep gorge of granite. It proves to be the most challenging aspect of our hike. Horsted and I puzzle over the best way to maneuver through it. After a few false starts, it becomes evident that there are only two routes: either wade or swim through a deep pool, or take

the high road over the top of the rocky neck. After a hazardous climb up two hundred feet of gravelly talus, we go over the top.

Our reward is a falcon's view of high, winding canyon walls with stunted juniper shading small pools of brown-tinted water.

High ridges funnel creek waters towards the plains at the eastern edge of Custer State Park.

Bur oak leaves glow yellow and green in the fall sunshine.

It is a tableau of rugged, magnificent isolation.

The descent down the opposite side is not as steep as the ascent, but is nonetheless treacherous. I end up glissading down part of the slope, grabbing pine saplings for brakes before reaching the streamside again.

Below the Narrows, both sides of the stream are steep and thickly wooded with shrubs and undergrowth. To avoid the brush, I walk down the middle of the knee-deep stream, which flows over rough cobbles. Near the south bank a small mallard duckling, too young to be out on its own, skitters across the water. On the bank, an empty nest in the tall grass, feathered with duck down, tells me where it was hatched. Near the nest a pile of hen feathers indicates the site of a struggle; now I know why the duckling is alone and confused.

About a half-mile below the Narrows, a

series of lovely waterfalls and pools appear. One of the pools is deep enough to swim in, and I use it to this advantage. The water is cold and refreshing. Below the pool, the canyon walls continue high and curved while the streambed is strewn with great boulders. In many places it takes total concentration to "boulder" over the rocks and not twist an ankle, and in many instances, poison ivy literally covers every available place to put a foot down.

A few miles farther, the canyon's granite gives way to the softer sedimentary Black Hills formations. The appearance of sedimentary rock marks the eastern edge of the Black Hills and signals our impending approach to the mouth of the canyon. Another indication of our descent is the change in riparian vegetation. We have moved from a mixed forest of spruce, pine, and birch to a hot, arid stretch dominated by pine. With the drop in elevation, more typical lowland trees, such as cottonwood, ash, and box elder, begin to appear. They are like old friends.

The stream flow also seems to be diminishing slightly, although there are still

Two mature bighorn sheep rams pose majestically in a green meadow.

crossings where we wade through pools and trenches up to our thighs. At a place where a cave pocks the smooth, high limestone face of the Madison formation, we pick up the trail that comes in from the east end of the

By midsummer, much of the lower stretch of French Creek becomes bone dry; a heavy thunderstorm may fill the streambed again for a few days.

———

natural area. Small falcons with wings bent like boomerangs ride the updrafts. On the ground, two mature turkeys with their flock of chirping chicks flush from the brush and scatter in all directions.

Near the Lower French Creek campground, three yearling bighorn sheep ewes graze the fresh green grass in the canyon's shade. Their light, buff-colored coats render them nearly imperceptible against the rock and dappled shade of the trees. They pay no attention to us.

About a quarter-mile below the lower campground, French Creek crosses the great Madison limestone formation and disappears into the streambed. During the summer, most of the small streams in the Black Hills promptly seep away at the base of the Madison and disappear into the stream gravel.

The noticeable dip of the sedimentary beds at the eastern top of the canyon gives notice that we are fast approaching the mouth of French Creek Canyon and the end of the trail. The Minnelusa formation with its corn yellows and rusty reds, now closer and lower, is burnished in the late afternoon sunlight. It is a welcome change from the massive walls of dull, gray granite.

French Creek has become a dry gulch.

We walk down the middle of its bleached cobble back. The riparian forest is now comprised primarily of broad-leafed trees: box elder, ash, bur oak, birch, and a few ghostly white skeletons of American elm. Under the cool canopy, lying at the edge of the streambed, a ribbon garter snake relaxes in the shade. I take its picture and admire the gloss of its scales.

As we approach the canyon's mouth, the floodplain opens up and flattens out to welcome the offerings of the prairie. Dominating the flat are blue vervain, coneflowers, tall vetch, and little bluestem. Large bur oaks shade the dry creekbed, while the pines have retreated to the slopes. On the rockiest, driest slopes, junipers join mountain mahogany in claiming this arid, scorching environment.

Our sojourn down French Creek is nearly over. Around the next bend lies the trailhead parking lot, and just beyond it are the vermilion cutbanks of the Red Valley. We started at 8:40 in the morning, and it is now 5:40 in the afternoon. In nine hours we covered twelve miles, making a slow descent from 4,700 feet to 3,700 feet. We have waded across French Creek more than fifty times, and hiked through what may be the world's longest winding patch of poison ivy.

My feet ache from slogging the last eight miles over boulders and stream cobbles in wet leather boots. Although we are tired and thirsty, it was a great trip through a rocky piece of paradise.

A grasshopper sits atop a pale purple coneflower along the cutbanks of the Red Valley.

BIGHORN SHEEP

The Audubon bighorn sheep, a subspecies of the Rocky Mountain bighorn sheep, once ranged across the northern plains west of the Missouri River. Due to their ability to graze the driest, most abrasive plants and their preference for precipitous areas, these animals were most often encountered in relatively inhospitable terrain. The Audubon bighorn is believed to have been exterminated in the Black Hills about 1895.

In 1922, eight Rocky Mountain bighorn sheep were introduced into Custer State Park. This initial population grew to 150 animals. In 1959, a die-off decimated the

population. In 1964, a second re-introduction of 22 animals from Wyoming was made. This population grew and currently stands at about 150 animals.

X

$\mathcal{W}$ IND *and* SKY

Wind and sky, sunlight and grass; the prairie extends to the horizon.

$\mathcal{I}$t is wind and sky. It is sunlight and grass. Appearing vast and limitless, the prairie possesses the inherent ability to blur lines, alter shapes, and change colors, mystifying and amazing the observer. What ultimately gives the prairie dimension are the birds, insects, flowers, and animals.

The south end of Custer State Park is such a prairie. More specifically, it is a transition zone where the prairie of the northern plains meets the ragged, pine-clad edge of the Black Hills. Here, the grass rules. Only on the ridges do pines stand guard while the swales and draws support a thin, winding ribbon of ash and oak.

Most of the prairie in Custer State Park is far removed from the dark forest canopies and the wind-sculpted granite spires. One must poke around in the waving grass to find this part of the park's subtleties—small songbirds, reptiles, insects, and discreet flowers. There are herds of powerful bison, curious pronghorn, and shy elk. Hawks and eagles circle low ridges while coyotes prowl the draws. Acre for acre, a healthy, native prairie harbors a wider diversity of plant and animal life than any other sort of natural area in North America.

Here, along the Prairie Trail in Custer State Park, little bluestem grass dominates and sets the tone for a classic mixed-grass prairie community. The mixed or midgrass prairie is a transition type between the tall grass prairie to the east, and the short grass prairies farther west.

Climbing up the first rise, I walk atop a substratum of Madison limestone. It supports familiar flower faces of leadplant, yellow coneflower, white and fringed sage, yellow cinquefoil, wavy-leaf thistle, and prickly pear cactus. Flitting about are small brown and dun-colored birds whose song and darting flight animate the grasslands. The birds are vesper, grasshopper, and chipping sparrows, hard to distinguish by sight. Their songs define their species and their place on the plains. More colorful, with a pale yellow breast patch and a sweet song, is the horned lark, one of the most common prairie birds. The meadowlark's chortling lilt, after a long winter's absence, is the joy of a prairie spring.

Leaving the rocky face of the Madison, the trail ascends to a high flat. With the presence of more topsoil over the rock, there

A blooming prickly pear cactus brings color to the prairie in June.

*A western meadowlark scans
the prairie horizon.*

is an evident change in fertility: the little bluestem is thicker, the leadplant taller and fuller. The spiked, stalked flowers of blue vervain shade from blue to purple. There are varieties of milkweed, their leaves waxy and fleshy with domed, drooping clusters of flowers in subtle shades of white, dusty rose, lavender, and magenta.

Here too, the prickly pears are large and succulent, sporting big yellow blossoms perched on the edge of pulpy, bristling pads in an effort to attract pollinating insects. Here is the silver scurfpea, which smells like gum, and the incredibly small, delicate, fuchsia blossoms of prairie clover. There are purple spiderworts with long, slender leaves, elegant

white sego lilies, velvet-stemmed psoralea, vetches of all shades and colors, and the common and beautiful wild pink prairie roses. South Dakota's native prairie flower propagator, Claude Barr, loved their pure, deep colors and referred to them as "jewels of the plains."

Not far off the trail, a female mountain bluebird, feathered in shades of soft turquoise and gray, perches in the lower branches of a large pine next to her birdhouse. Inside are two eggs. She flies in so close I can almost touch her.

Beyond the pine, some fifty feet away, a pronghorn buck stands motionless in the grass. I catch a whiff of his musty scent. He watches me curiously.

Straying east off the trail leads me to a thin row of pines growing along a ledge of pink Minnekahta limestone. Below, at the foot of the ridge, grows a plum thicket. Nearby, a few old stone foundations and a springhouse are sheltered by huge cottonwoods. Known as the old Korthaus homestead, it harbors a sense of serenity that belongs to another era.

Beyond the springhouse, five young pronghorn bucks spar, cavort, and race across a smooth, green draw. It is a privilege to watch them at play. For a moment they all stop to gaze in my direction. Since the outline of my shape is broken by the pines, they are unable to conclusively identify me. Following their curious instinct, they eventually circle around the ridge to catch my scent and come directly to face me. Pronghorns are among the most curious and nervous wild animals on the plains. When spooked they move in unison like a school of tropical fish.

I walk down the spine of the ridge, cross the spring-fed creek, and climb onto the back of another pine-studded ridge to Hay Flats. This flat area is a wide little bluestem prairie speckled with yellow coneflowers and pink roses and framed under a hard blue sky.

Turning back to the west I drop down into the shelter of oak and ash trees that line the banks of Flynn Creek. Shade is always a blessing on the prairie in the hot afternoon, and water is the gift of life. I cross Flynn Creek near its mouth and walk along the edge

An old springhouse stands as a historic reminder of the Korthaus homestead.
Photo by Greg Goebel.

Prairie dogs bask and feed near their burrow on the prairie at the edge of the Black Hills.

of the trees bordering Lame Johnny Creek.

Lame Johnny's is an interesting tale. His given name was Cornelius Donahue. He received his nickname when, as a child, he injured a leg in a fall from a horse. Along with a partner who went by the interesting sobriquet of Limping Jesus, he took up a squatter's homestead on the creek that now bears his name. Johnny was well educated and had at times worked as an accountant. But when he came west he developed an unfortunate interest in livestock rustling and stagecoach robbery, making him unpopular with the more law-abiding frontier folk. His larcenous misdeeds finally caught up with him, and he was apprehended in Pine Ridge in early fall of 1878.

En route to Deadwood for trial, the stagecoach carrying Lame Johnny was ambushed north of Buffalo Gap. Shackled in leg irons, Johnny was unceremoniously removed by unknown parties and hanged from a cottonwood tree near the creek that bears his name. Here he chose to live, and here, by his own misdeeds, as it poetically turned out, he died.

Much has been left here along the park's Prairie Trail: old homesteads, old names, and old stories. It all lends a certain character to this country that waves in the wind, shimmers in the heat, and rises to fly in the sky with the morning sun. ❧

Pronghorn

The American Pronghorn, often called an antelope, is not related to any members of the antelope group. In fact, the pronghorn is an animal unique to North America.

Having evolved on the flat, wide-open western plains, the pronghorn has the keenest vision of any American mammal. It can see a small object in motion up to four miles away. It also possesses great speed and can run for an extended period of time at forty to fifty miles per hour. Its large lungs and oversized heart allow it to run at these high speeds without taxing its circulatory system.

By 1908, the vast pronghorn herds that had once inhabited the Great Plains had been reduced to a mere twenty thousand animals. Due to concerted efforts to preserve them as a species, their numbers have since increased dramatically in the West and even stabilized. In 1916, a dozen bottle-raised pronghorns were introduced into Custer State Park. Few of these human-raised animals survived long enough to reproduce, and more experimentation had to take place before their reintroduction was finally successful. Today a relatively small but stable herd of pronghorns roams the park's prairie.

On the prairie near the Wildlife Loop Road, a young

pronghorn nuzzles its mother.

Two bison calves follow their mothers across a prairie sunrise.

$\mathscr{P}$TE OYATE

A bison at rest.

$\mathscr{P}$*te Oyate* means "Buffalo Nation" in Lakota. Perhaps no other creature captures the spirit and essence of life on the western Great Plains as does the American bison, which once roamed here in numbers beyond comprehension. Herds covering twenty to fifty square miles with four million animals were not uncommon.

Parts of these great bison herds migrated seasonally, moving to the south in winter, then back to their summer ranges on the northern plains. In the spring, the herds broke into smaller units consisting of cow and calf pairs and yearling groups, along with bachelor herds of bulls. The groups scattered to forage, moving continuously, day-by-day, stopping to ruminate and rest in the afternoon and in the darkness. Bison of today

still do most of their intensive grazing in the early morning and late afternoon. Midday is their time for resting, chewing their cuds, and wallowing.

A ponderously regal bison bull can weigh a ton, stand six feet high at the shoulders, and stretch more than eleven feet from head to rear. Bison cows are somewhat smaller and weigh less; a good-sized calf can tip the scales at three hundred pounds by its first autumn.

As creatures conditioned by the rigors of the last Ice Age, bison are exceptionally hardy and have the ability to withstand extremes of heat, cold, and drought. When excited, they quickly break into a lumbering gallop and can run at a top speed of thirty-five miles per hour. Despite their enormous size and bulk, bison are agile enough to quickly swerve and turn when under attack or pursued.

Thirty-six American bison were introduced into Custer State Park in 1914. Since then, the herd has steadily increased. By the early 1940s, the number had grown to two thousand animals. Today the number of Custer State Park bison has been stabilized at a winter herd of nine hundred animals; each spring, an additional five hundred calves are born. Following a fall roundup, the surplus live animals are sold at auction, and a handful of mature bison bulls are removed from the herd each year through harvest hunting.

Because of their size and presence, bison attract the most attention in the park. On one occasion, I stopped to admire and photo-

Cowbirds pluck insects from a bison's shaggy coat.

*Cowpokes on
horseback keep the
bison herd moving
during the annual
fall roundup at
Custer State Park.*

graph a bachelor herd of old bulls in Barnes Canyon, being particularly interested in getting a picture of a buffalo bird, also known as a cowbird, dexterously employed in gleaning insects from the great beasts' hides. It was a rainy, drizzly morning, and my patience gave out before I got the shot I wanted.

Walking back to the truck I watched another great bull wade into a creek to drink. I came within 10 yards of him before he stopped to take a long look at me. He gave me a hard, no-nonsense, penetrating stare. I understood at that moment what Les

Ducheneaux, as guardian and ceremonial slaughterer of the Cheyenne River Sioux bison herd, meant when he said, "When the Creator made the buffalo, he put a power in them." Ducheneaux was referring to their ability to sustain and heal two-legged creatures. Beyond that, I also clearly felt the bull's great physical power and intense focus.

When the bull turned his head away from me, I could hear his deep, labored breathing and feel his great strength as he pulled first one front leg, then the other out of knee-deep creek mud. There was the

A reddish-colored bison calf sticks close to its mother.

distinct sucking sound of greasy muck as he climbed out. Standing on the bank in the wet grass, he turned again and took notice of me. The great brown eye peering from his huge, black, bushy-haired face held a sense of calm and detached confidence that was absolutely devoid of fear. The message was unmistakable. He was in control; this was his turf, and I was an intruder of no consequence. I felt humble and stood dead still. All I could think was, "Ho kola, Pte oyate."

A lone bull bison browses through a forested glade on a foggy spring morning.

Some of the 1,400 bison in Custer State Park move across the expanse of grasslands near the park's eastern border.

Spring

The brightest of the seasons is spring, who delights in wearing delicate, pastel raiment and richly scented perfumes; rain, flowing water, and thunder are music to her ears.

Summer

Summer arrives luxuriously outfitted in soft, deep greens and warm, strong, earthy scents; she languishes in tall, waving grass and the warm breath of the south wind on a long, simmering afternoon.

Fall

Fall creeps in behind summer's green curtain, ceremoniously attiring herself in ritual garments of bronze, red, and gold to ponder the achievements of spring and summer before finally giving way to her majesty, winter.

Winter

Lady Winter, with shoulders bare above her flowing gown of glistening whiteness, presides over long nights filled with cold, lustrous moonlight, dark shadows, and dreams of deep and quiet repose.

Two bison graze on the snow-covered prairie of Custer State Park.

XII

THE SEASON *of* REPOSE: BISON & ELK

A bison's thick coat
protects it from winter's cold.

ison

On a winter afternoon, a small cow-calf herd of bison occupies a terrace on the south side of Lost Canyon Draw. Getting a closer look means crunching through knee-high snowdrifts and up the bur oak-lined gully. When I am opposite the herd, I make my way up to the edge of the gully and stand behind a large bison-scarred pine. The herd is small—about sixty animals, most of which are standing quietly fifty yards away.

My movements are immediately detected by four young heifers in the front who look up and watch me curiously. Behind them, most of the other animals are actively engaged in brushing away snow with their great snouts and grabbing meager mouthfuls of dry grass. A half-dozen are lying down, ruminating. The heifers and I stand looking

A group of bison continues to graze, paying no attention to the falling snow.

at each other across the silent snow. Slowly the herd begins to rouse itself. Somewhere, unnoticed by me, an old lead cow, perhaps reacting to my presence, has given the signal to move. Those lying down are getting up; those standing or grazing are shifting position and perambulating at an easy gait up and out of the draw.

I back down a few feet into the shelter of the gully, using the oaks to break up my form. The heifers all turn away. Responding to the herd instinct, they too begin to amble slowly up the hillside. Behind me, the wind picks up, swirling hard crystals of snow that sting my face. I drop back down to the floor of the gully to shelter myself from its bite.

Sawing through the oaks, an occasional

hard wind gust rattles dry, brittle leaves above me. On the north edge of the gully, wands of tall, blond grass bend at the wind's insistence. Somewhere in the distance a crow caws twice, then twice again. A pair of horned larks chirp sweetly above me before flying off together to the southwest. Feeling refreshed and warmer, I climb to the top of the gully and look south into the sun. The bison have all disappeared.

I walk to where they were standing. Interspersed amid crisscrossed trails are piles of fresh dung, brushed areas where they plowed away the snow to get to the grass, and holes in the snow half-filled with frozen slush where a warm bison body recently lay. I follow their meandering trails south out of the draw. I note track sizes, depths of various trails in the snow, freshness of excrement, general direction of movement and wind. I experience a primal adrenaline rush. I am hunting; I have become a predator. My whole body knows this. My senses are all flushed and heightened to a single instinct: find and move up to the bison herd for the kill. How many hundreds of generations before me followed the trails of wild animals, first as hunters intent on the kill, and later as herders? The veneer of twentieth-century civilization is so thin and short compared to the long centuries of excitement connected to the chase and the kill.

Above the draw a quarter-mile south, the bison are grazing at the edge of a copse of pine, heads down in snow-covered grass, their cinnamon brown backs and rears to the wind. I am at their backs and methodically move up to their downwind flanks, the preferred position of a hunter not wishing or able to employ an ambuscade from the trees. None take notice of me.

A broad line of cirrus clouds, acting like an opaque lens, slides in front of the sun, darkening the snow. The bison, their hides now a deeper tone of brown, are all standing next to the backdrop of ponderosa. The darkened tonal quality of their bodies blends so closely with that of the curtain of pines it renders them almost invisible. Only their movements betray them.

They keep moving, and I follow, closing the distance to fifty yards. I gain their downwind flanks. A few stop to peer at me, their wide, dark, curly-haired faces flecked with snow. Once, *tatanka,* we praised, sang, danced, hunted, and partook of your spirit and flesh. Now we can only contemplate you: our loss. I watch the wind kick up a swirling snow devil that passes between us before turning away, breaking off the hunt and crunching my way back through finger drifts of snow to Lost Canyon Draw.

Elk

It is just before six in the morning, near the time of the winter solstice. A bright, enormous, and benign full moon hangs over the pines on the west side of Jolly Flats. The sheen of its silvery light washes across the snow-blanketed prairie. At first light I catch sight of an elk herd grazing an east-facing slope below the moon at the edge of the timber. From the road in the twilight, at a distance of about a half-mile, they appear as small, reddish brown dots against the snow.

Slowly, working my way up a side draw and using its oaks for cover, I manage to get within close range of the herd. It is a cow and calf group of about one hundred. The morning light gives their buff-colored rumps a dark hue of rusty brown. They are beautiful: shy, quiet, timid, and gentle. Most are bunched close together and grazing in a desultory fashion. Occasionally I hear a mew or soft whistle. As I kneel in the snow, hidden behind a boulder seventy-five yards from them, they are unaware of my presence.

At 7:15, direct sunlight hits the top of the pines and starts to creep down the hillside toward the grazing elk. When the light strikes the herd, they stop feeding. As if on cue, their heads rise, and they slowly walk into the timber. Those farthest away and highest on the hill, mainly young bulls with spiked antlers, are the last to turn and trot down the hill in single file into the forest. In less than three minutes, they have all disappeared into the timber with hardly a sound.

I walk up to their grazing area to look at their leavings—piles of pellets, a few melted oval elk beds in the snow, and elegant tracks consisting of two symmetrical crescents opposite each other. When put together, these cloven hoof prints are the size of my hand.

On the sidehill where the young bulls grazed, I rest under a large ponderosa pine amid cones and dried red tufts of little bluestem. The sun is rising, stirring the wind. Occasionally I hear a low whistle behind me in the timber. East across Jolly Flats, the crisscross meanderings of elk trails punctuating the snow are now clearly visible in the morning light. ❄

A bull elk will carry his antlers through the fall mating season; they will drop off during the winter.

Photo by Mark Kayser.

E L K

In 1888, the last elk native to the Black Hills was shot and killed. This particular subspecies, known as the Manitoban elk, was once extremely abundant over the Great Plains. The elk species found in the park today is the Rocky Mountain elk, a forest dweller native to high Rocky Mountains. Rocky Mountain elk from Idaho and Wyoming were reintroduced into Custer State Park in 1913.

Elk are members of the deer family. As herd animals, they instinctively move in groups, except when calving. In the park there are about five major sub-herds, which average about 175 to 200 animals each. These sub-herds are further broken down into smaller units that consist of young bulls, older bulls, and cow/calf groups.

In summer there is a good deal of elk movement between these various groups within the park. During this time of year, most elk groups intensively use the burn areas. They generally prefer to spend daylight hours high on rocky ridges and to move down to lower meadows and burn areas for water and grazing in the evening and at night.

In September, for a period of four to six weeks, bull elk gather mating harems during what is called the "rut." With the onset of winter, the bulls again segregate, and with cow and calf herds, leave the high country and gravitate to the open prairies on the east side of the park. ❄

Prior to the Galena fire of 1988, elk numbers in Custer State Park were maintained at about 550 animals. The fire, which burned nearly seventeen thousand acres of forest in the park, created new grassland habitat attractive to these large grazers. Due to the increased forage area, the elk population is increasing. Custer State Park's target for ideal elk management is 1,000 animals.

Mountain lions roam the Black Hills, but the elk's most persistent natural predator, the wolf, no longer exists in this forest ecosystem. To compensate for the absence of this important predator, a certain number of elk hunting licenses are issued annually to trim the herd, keeping it in balance with Custer State Park's capacity to maintain forage and habitat.

XIII

A POET'S PATH

"... With mountains of green all around me
and mountains of white up above
And mountains of blue down the sky-line,
I follow the trail that I love."

~Badger Clark, The Old Prospector

Badger Clark's cabin,
the Badger Hole.

*I*n the heart of Custer State Park, a small cabin constructed of native timber and stone perches on a hillside above Galena Creek. Nicknamed the "Badger Hole" by its builder, Charles Badger Clark, Jr., it has in its own way become a legacy and testament to a man who chose to live the simple life surrounded by the beauty of nature.

It was the last day of August when I stopped at the Badger Hole to visit with Badger's grandniece, Phyllis Schwartz. The morning was drizzly and cold; clouds of mist hid and encircled the mountains, and everything dripped with moisture. After a hot, dry summer in the Black Hills, the rain was a welcome relief. A taste of fall was in the air and while a few trees hinted at gold, it was the singsong melody of chickadees in the dripping, rain-slick forest that announced it.

The sense of peace and tranquillity that surrounds Badger Clark's old cabin is profound enough to be clearly palpable. Inside, Phyllis Schwartz sat in an old chair against a wall of books, ready to greet visitors. Schwartz is the granddaughter of Badger's oldest brother, Hal. Having grown up intimately associated with Clark, the former poet laureate of South Dakota, she carefully tends his memory in her retirement.

Charles Badger Clark, Jr., was born in Albia, Iowa, in 1883. Three months later his father, a Methodist minister, moved his wife and three sons to a homestead four miles south of Plankinton, Dakota Territory. The family lived in eastern South Dakota during most of Clark's childhood, eventually moving to Deadwood in 1898, where his mother passed

away that same year from tuberculosis.

In 1901, Clark's father married Anna Morris. It was she who later encouraged Badger to write poems.

After graduating from Deadwood High School in 1902, Charles Badger Clark went on to Dakota Wesleyan College, where he studied for a year before going to Cuba with a group of idealists who were interested in starting a commune. The social experiment failed, and Clark returned to South Dakota in 1905. At the age of twenty-two, he contracted tuberculosis, the disease that had already claimed his mother and his brother Fred. In 1906, hoping to arrest the disease in a warmer, drier climate, he moved to Tombstone, Arizona.

Shortly after his arrival, Bob "Spike" Axtell took a liking to young Badger Clark and gave him a job on the ranch he managed. Within months, the young man was cured. He stayed on the ranch for four years, relishing the beauty of the Southwest and absorbing the lifestyle of a cowboy. He taught himself to play guitar and sing, and he started writing poetry.

It was during this time that Anna Morris sent one of his poems, entitled "Ridin," to *Pacific Monthly Magazine*. The poem was accepted, and Badger was surprised to receive the princely sum of ten dollars for his effort. Later, he described that check as "the greenest money I ever made." He continued writing and selling more poetry to

Badger Clark's distinctive dress showed the independence and mystery of this bigger-than-life man.

Courtesy South Dakota State Historical Society.

the magazine.

In 1910, Clark moved to Hot Springs, South Dakota, with his parents, bringing his newfound love of the open range and the outdoors with him. Upon returning to the Black Hills, he became engaged for a second time to his former fiancée, Helen Fowler, but it was a romance and engagement that never bloomed and Clark would remain a bachelor throughout his life.

During this period Clark's father's health failed and the young poet helped care for him while continuing to write. Badger Clark also joined the Chautauqua circuit, speaking at public events around the state and region. Being in front of large audiences unnerved him at first, but he soon came to enjoy his speaking engagements. Although his work earned him only five to seven hundred dollars per year, it gave him the freedom necessary to care for his father, write, and roam the Black Hills.

In 1921, Clark's father died. Six years later, Badger Clark scouted out a place to live in Custer State Park and eventually received permission from the state to build a small, one-room cabin above Galena Creek, south of Legion Lake. Here, for the better part of a decade, Badger lived with only a bed, a table, three chairs, a wood stove — and seven

Willows frame a fog-shrouded Legion Lake not far from the Badger Hole.

hundred books. His lifestyle was reminiscent of the New England transcendentalist Henry David Thoreau, who wrote a century earlier in his most well-known book, *Walden,* "I went to the woods because I wished to live deliberately, to front only the essential facts of life, and see if I could not learn what it had to teach, and not, when I came to die, discover that I had not lived."

In 1937, Badger's stepmother, Anna Morris Clark, passed away, leaving him a small inheritance. With the money, Badger constructed a new cabin near his old one, using beautiful native quartz, schists, and mica-flecked granites he hauled from nearby Galena Creek. He furnished the cabin with

the soft couches, chairs, and rockers that his folks had used. As the years passed, Badger continued to make numerous public appearances, write on a number of topics of a philosophical and political nature, and give poetry readings across the state. He dressed in distinctive military fashion for all his formal engagements. His outfit included a narrow-brimmed silver-belly hat, a khaki wool military jacket, breeches, high military boots, a white shirt, and a black silk scarf as a tie.

Badger Clark's living room also served as his library and writing study. The back wall is lined entirely with books, mostly the classics of English and American literature.

While he preferred to live simply, immersed in nature, he drank deeply from the founts of learning. He owned complete collections of Shakespeare, Kipling, Twain, Browning, O. Henry, the Harvard Classics, and the Encyclopedia Britannica, along with works by Chaucer, Bacon, Keats, Lamb, Voltaire, and many others. He also had a taste for history, geography, and archaeology.

For me, sitting in his kitchen at his old dining table, writing notes on this poet's life was easy and natural. His rustic home is a writer's retreat. Outside, seen through a window at the end of the table, lay the woods full of deer, bison, birds, and small animals that Clark loved; inside were the simple comforts of an old wood stove, iron skillets, spice tins, crockery bowls, tarnished silverware, and an assortment of old china plates, cups, saucers, and pitchers. Throughout the kitchen lingers the warmth of another era when life was more relaxed and hospitable.

In 1957, at the age of seventy-four, Badger Clark died. "We didn't know he was sick," said his grandniece Phyllis, "until a couple of weeks before he died. He never complained, even at the end." In recollecting her great-uncle, Schwartz described him as a lovable person who spent the holidays with her family. "When we came out to visit him in the summer, his home and the area around it was like a playground. He let us get away with murder here; he never scolded us. I never knew him to be cross or to use angry words. He was always glad to see us.

Hoarfrost decorates an oak leaf still clinging to a branch in mid-winter.

I can still see him sometimes reading poetry, playing the guitar, and singing for us in the house. He was one of the kindest men I've ever known."

It is time to leave. Outside, the mist has grown heavier. It seems an appropriate time to walk the mile-long memorial trail Clark built and frequently used up to the ridge behind his cabin. The late afternoon woods are calm and muted with soft rain. A flicker chirps once in the distance. There are deer tracks in the mud. A thrush watches me, then moves quietly through the understory. The trail winds through thickets of saplings richly festooned with mint-colored lichens and old man's beard. Along the way, chipmunks scurry and animate ancient outcroppings of lichen-covered granite.

Along the ridge, a breeze moves gently through the wet pines. Across the Galena valley, the mountains and trees are cloud-hidden, wreathed in fog and mist. Standing in the midst of short pines, watching the clouds drape down over the mountains, I experience a poignant sense of peace and serenity I want to give myself up to. The path I walk is clearly laid out by a poet for seekers of the spirit.

I contemplate Clark's unpublished 1948 New Year's Day poem, written on a postcard featuring a black-and-white portrait of himself.

From his porch, Badger Clark reflects on his surroundings.

Courtesy South Dakota State Historical Society.

New Year's Day 1948

Another birthday, and I glide
This Year across a grim divide
Passing from elderly to old,
From autumn ripe to winter cold.
My years, my years, O sorry sum!
So many gone, so few to come,
So many words that I have said,
So many books that I have read,
So many friends among the dead
All day behind, all dusk ahead!

And yet I haven't gone so far
But what my eyes can see a star,
Or blue flame of a jay in flight
Or winter woods bedecked in white
Or black pine on a rising moon,
And I yet hear the pensive tune
Of frozen brooks in hidden flow
Singing away beneath the snow,
And my old blood is not too old
To dance a jig to piping cold.
Count in a book, a song, a walk
And friendly laughter, easy talk
And work, though freely I declare
I haven't much to add on there.
Yes, it's good fun to be alive
Even if I'm sixty-five.

Closer to the end of his life, again pondering his mortality, Badger wrote another poem, entitled "I Must Come Back," in which he extols the beauty of this wondrous park and his deep attachment to the Black Hills. But it is a handful of lines from his poem, "Old-Timer," that haunts me as I walk over his beloved trail back to the house.

> *"Old-timer friend, the trails you wend are*
> *mostly dim and grassed:*
> *Your talk meanders lazily through*
> *valleys of the past..."*
>
> ~Badger Clark,
> Old-Timer

About the Author

Edward Raventon is a freelance writer and photographer who regularly contributes feature stories and articles about the American West for regional magazines and newspapers. For seven years, he served as chief interpreter and naturalist for the South Dakota Division of Parks and Recreation. He teaches creative writing and lives in the Black Hills. His first book, *Island in the Plains: A Black Hills Natural History*, was published in 1994.

The author with Countless, on the edge of the high plains.

ABOUT THE PHOTOGRAPHER

Paul Horsted has spent much of the past 15 years photographing South Dakota's people, places, and natural beauty. Early in his career, he worked as a staff photographer at the Sioux Falls *Argus Leader*; after graduating from South Dakota State University in Brookings, he served as Chief Photographer for the South Dakota Department of Tourism.

Mr. Horsted left that position to start his own business, and presently works as a freelance nature and travel photographer. His specialties include time-exposure photographs of natural phenomena such as star trails and lightning storms; between exposures, he enjoys lecturing about the art of photography, and doing slide shows of his past projects.

Mr. Horsted's publication credits include books on South Dakota, Mt. Rushmore, and Badlands National Park. His photographs have also appeared in such magazines as *LIFE, National Geographic, Travel-Holiday,* and *Reader's Digest.*

Black Hill Parks and Forests Association

The Black Hills Parks and Forests Association supports
interpretive programs, educational activities and research
in an effort to protect and preserve the cultural and
natural resources of the Black Hills.

You, too, can help support the interpretive activities of the affiliated
parks and forests in the Black Hills by joining the Black Hills Parks
and Forests Association, a nonprofit organization dedicated to
enhancing the experiences of visitors to the Black Hills.

For information about the Black Hills Parks and Forests Association
and how you can become a member, please contact:

Black Hills Parks and Forests Association
Rt. 1 Box 190
Wind Cave National Park
Hot Springs, SD 57747
605-745-7020

Custer State Park
HC 83 Box 70
Custer, SD 57730
605-255-4515